Menopause Survival Manual
for Men

John C. Winters

Printed in the U.S.A. by
BookMasters, Inc.
30 Amberwood Parkway
P.O. Box 388
Ashland, OH 44805
1-800-537-6727

ISBN-10: 0-9787218-0-2
ISBN-13: 978-0-9787218-0-0

Dedication

*This book is dedicated
to my sons, Ernie and Joshua;
my son-in-law, Jeff;
and my two grandsons, Avery and Ryan,
who will all one day be living in hurricane
country.*

I also want to thank my wife for giving me the menopause…I mean, the *material* to write this book. Believe it or not, my wife is the one who told me I ought to write a book about how men can survive menopause. She said it would be a best-seller.

It all started with ice. I just had surgery on my knee and was stuck in a reclining chair for a week. I needed a steady supply of ice to be brought upstairs to go on my knee. Well, on about the third day after surgery, I asked for ice one too many times.

And that's when she said I needed to write a book.

I want recognize the hundreds of thousands of people who were affected by the hurricanes that hit the U.S. in 2005. The first draft of this book was written before any of those events, and I delayed publishing this book out of respect for the people who endured them. Although this book uses hurricanes in a humorous, fictional way, it is in no way meant to minimize or make fun of their real impact on human life. In fact, it is quite the opposite. As a result of the research I did for this book, my understanding of hurricanes has given me even more respect and admiration for the people who brave these storms because they have nowhere else to go, and for the people who risk their lives trying to bring a better understanding to these events. My hat is off to the true hurricane fighters and survivors!

I am indebted to the following organizations: the National Weather Service, the National Oceanic and Atmospheric Administration, and the Hurricane Research Division of the Atlantic Oceanographic and Meteorological Laboratory. Their websites have been invaluable resources to me.

Medical Disclaimer
I am not a doctor, and I have no medical training or clinical medical experience. The procedures and medications I have discussed in this book are presented from my own point of view, concerning my wife's journey through menopause. The incidents and information in this book are intended for entertainment, not medical diagnosis. Please seek advice from your physician if you or your spouse experience any symptoms which might be related to menopause.

Table of Contents

Introduction:
Men on Pause

Over the years, my wife and I have learned that the best medicine for tough times is humor. The sooner we can joke about things, the better.

And then we ran into menopause. Or it ran into us. I'm not sure who ran into whom. I'm not sure it really matters. But here we are, six years into this, and as you will see as you turn the pages, humor has helped to get us through. (Well, at least it has greased the skids a little so I don't get as many splinters in my behind.)

Okay. Let me try and get serious. This book is about a serious topic, one that has wrecked many a woman's mid-life, many a man's mid-life, and many 20+ year marriages, not to mention the collateral damage to kids, pets, and bank accounts.

There seem to be as many books catering to women readers about menopause as there are variations of how women experience menopause. I guess that's why women differ on how long they go through menopause; it lasts until they find the book

1

that describes precisely how they are going through it, and then they can be cured. (My wife is still looking for her book. I hope she finds it soon.)

The first book my wife brought home was titled something like, *Menopause: The Silent Passage*. I don't know who the person was that wrote that book, but I sure have not seen anything silent about menopause (unless you are referring to the "1001st way to use Duct Tape".)

But I have yet to find a book that helps *men* get through menopause. I am becoming convinced that it's really us men who are going through the "silent passage" of menopause; no one has written about us, and no one is talking about us. If life is like a box of chocolates, then a man's experience with menopause is like...well, use your imagination! We men need some guidance FAST on how in the world we are to survive menopause.

Just like women's books (where you have to keep looking until you find the right one, or perhaps some complex formula made up from lots of different books), it might take thousands of other brave men who will risk the ire of their menopausal spouses to share their struggles in the midst of their storms. But I'll give this my best shot. Perhaps our generation can come out of this better off than some of our predecessors, who, incidentally, left us with no instructions on how to handle this mess. I don't know, maybe they were just too shell-shocked to share with us how they made it through because they were suffering from post-traumatic menopause syndrome. (Hey, is there a non-narcotic medication for that?) Or maybe they wanted to watch us endure the same things they had gone through, the twisted logic being that they could get back at the mother of *their* children by letting her male offspring suffer.

I chose to use the illustration of a hurricane season to describe my experiences with menopause in memory of my father (and because of the eerie similarities between the two events). I remembered what my dad told me about hurricanes. Before the equal rights movement, they were always named after women. My dad told me that was because women are always unpredictable. You see, by that time, my dad had gone through a "Category 5" menopause with two different wives, so he knew what he was talking about. A tornado might be more destructive at its most powerful point of contact, but tornadoes usually last only a few minutes. Hurricanes can go on for days, and a hurricane season for months, which seems like an eternity compared to a tornado. At least with a tornado, you know the outcome really fast. You either make it, or you don't. And if you do, your stuff is either still there, or it isn't. With a hurricane, there is what seems to be an endless wait for the outcome. And then there's always the chance that another one is just around the corner.

Rather than just taking my dad's word about hurricanes, I actually looked up the history of naming hurricanes, since I wanted to confirm at least *some* historical legitimacy. One website reported that the first use of a proper name for a tropical cyclone was by an Australian forecaster early in the 20th century. He named storms after politicians he didn't like. Then, during WWII, U.S. military meteorologists began naming them after their wives and girlfriends. (Gee, I wonder why?) In 1979, the National Weather Service started using men's names, too. (Coincidence? Or just a product of the equal rights movement?)

I also wonder why the word "men" is in *men*opause. Maybe it's because we men are blazing through life, having just grasped our second wind after navigating through our own mid-life crisis. Then all of a sudden, we're blasted by some unknown force that comes out of nowhere. It stops us dead in our tracks. We are suddenly men on pause, dumbfounded, facing a series of life-storms that no one prepared us for. I guess that first book my wife bought (remember the *Silent Passage*?) really did have historical validity. No one ever used to talk about it, so no one was able to learn about it, or prepare for its destructive onslaught. Over the past few years, the silence has been broken for women. It's time that it was broken for men.

Menopause Survival Manual for Men

1

Why Live in Hurricane Country?

According to the National Oceanic and Atmospheric Administration, an average hurricane unleashes the power of a 10-megaton nuclear bomb every 20 minutes. The power of one average hurricane, if it could be tapped, could supply the entire world with electricity for a year. (Statistic for the year 1990)

Why do people choose to live in a place where, year after year, there is a real possibility that their home and possessions will be wiped off the face of the earth by an unstoppable force of water and wind?

You have probably seen this scenario on television. A reporter cannot resist the temptation to ask such a cutting question to some poor soul whose life has just been devastated. And much to my surprise—and probably yours as well—the person does *not* deck the news reporter with a strewn-about two-by-four, nor does he try to drown him in the six feet of water that is in his living room. Instead, he answers in a way that lets you know the person is in love with where he lives, for better or for worse, in good weather and in bad.

If you have ever traveled in hurricane country (which, in the U.S., is generally anywhere along the Atlantic coast, from North Carolina all the way around Florida and west to Texas), it is truly a beautiful place. You can find white, sandy beaches, and oceans whose waters are warm enough to bathe in almost year-round. (The warm water thing may not mean anything to you, unless you are from the west coast like me, where even in the summer, the waters off the coast of California are cold enough to shrink your manhood to the size of a child's.) This region boasts beautiful, semi-tropical plants and trees, and flowers whose colors burst out at you in their splendor. It is a mild climate for the most part, where snow is almost unheard of, and sunny days are the norm. People treasure the laid-back atmosphere, where sitting on a nice, big porch with a glass of lemonade or sweet tea on a hot summer day is almost like heaven.

Chapter 1: Why Live in Hurricane Country?

There is really only one drawback (besides the scathing humidity in July and August, or, if you live in Florida, those huge spiders and cockroaches). During any given summer or fall, the grim hurricane reaper may come calling on you to collect her tribute. She may come only for an offering of a few shingles or yard shrubs, or she may demand and take everything you have. That is the price you pay to live in a place many consider heaven on earth.

So why do men choose to marry and stay with women, who, once a month for years and years, unleash the equivalent of an emotional tornado, and then, in the middle of their life, switch over to the most formidable unleashing of energy the world has ever known?

I can't tell you why other men choose to live in "menopause country," but I can tell you why I do. My wife's vibrancy is more striking than a Florida sunrise. Her personality is more colorful than a garden full of the richest tropical flowers. Her thoughtfulness is more refreshing than a cool breeze and a tall glass of lemonade on a hot Alabama summer afternoon. Her caring attitude is more soothing than warm waves lapping up on the

Outer Banks on a cozy evening. For me, she is a taste of heaven on earth.

That's why I choose to live in hurricane country.

This chapter might have been a better fit toward the end of this book. However, I put it here because I wanted to give you an opportunity to reflect on all the wonderful reasons you married your wife. I wanted you to start this book out remembering why you married the person you did and knowing she is still that person deep inside.

As you read this book, you need to know and remember that a hurricane does not have a mind, a conscience, or feelings. Neither does menopause. You have to look at menopause as if your wife is having an "out-of-body" experience, or you will allow offense and hurt to come into your marriage that may become irreparable.

I know you will say to yourself, and possibly to your friends: "Come on, she HAS to have SOME control over this thing! It can't be THIS bad on its own! She HAS to be milking this thing, or trying to milk ME!" You know, up until about two years ago, I think I felt the same way. But then something happened to me physically that changed my attitude.

I had just come back from Southeast Asia, and had picked up some kind of stomach bug. Between the virus, the antibiotics the doctor gave me, *and* the half-dozen vaccinations I got before the trip, my thyroid gland was thrown off. I didn't realize just how much your thyroid controls until then. For those of us who never think about our thyroid, it is one of the major glands in your body that releases hormones to help regulate your body. My thyroid became "hyperactive," meaning it was giving out more hormones than it was supposed to. My resting heart rate became double what it should be. My metabolism increased so much that even though I ate like a pig, I lost 20 pounds of muscle mass in a month. My muscles were always working, even when I tried to rest. My mind and body did not know how to shut down. I couldn't sleep for an entire month. I was always tired, but couldn't rest. I became short-tempered and irritable at the smallest of things. I really wasn't myself.

Oh, my God—I sound like a woman going through menopause!

You get the point.

Menopause Survival Manual for Men

2

The Pre-Hurricane "Periods"

During our first few years of marriage, I never knew what each new month would bring, that is, when it was "that" time of the month. At first, I didn't know *why* what was happening was happening. (Hey, my dad raised my brother and me, so it was just three males...what can I say?) Once I made the connection that the unpredictable emotions came along with the unfamiliar items I had to pick up at the grocery store (*"Price check on Aisle 5 for tampons!"*), I started putting it all together. Then I figured if my wife was brazen enough to ask ME to buy those things, then I should be able to be bold enough to start asking her questions about this "special" time of the month. A few months later, I learned that timing was everything concerning "when" I should ask those questions.

Once I started to ask at the right times, and she started to answer, I figured out that she was always affected in one of a handful of ways, although we never knew which way until one day into it. Once we knew what we were in for, we knew we had just six more days to go, and then we were out of the storm for a good 21 days at least. Of course, if she was pregnant, we got a bonus, because we got to skip at least nine months. Now I see the wisdom that farmers had a few generations ago. The dads didn't want more kids to work the farm; they wanted more kids to get more of those nine-month reprieves. My grandfather on my dad's side was a lot smarter than I ever thought: he had eleven kids.

After about six months of marriage, I pretty much knew my wife's storm "menu"...

CRYING AND CLINGY

This was the period where she'd boo-hoo at everything. It reminded me of those re-runs of the *I Love Lucy* show where Lucy did that cry with her mouth wide open. Only my wife didn't quite cry like that. It was more of a "someone-died-that-wasn't-really-close, but-pretty-close" cry. Or like how women cry from one of those tear-jerker chick movies where even the guys get a little choked up, but try not to let on. She needed my shoulder to cry on, and that was it. That's okay for a tear-jerker movie once a week, but for a whole week it kinda gets old and cramps a guy's style. But I learned to be nice anyway, because if you're not, it makes it a whole lot worse when the bad periods hit. (I didn't know that at first, but I picked it up real fast.) I don't know how they store that stuff up and save it for the bad periods, but believe me, they do.

CRY...AND RUN AND HIDE

This is the one where at first I thought she just wanted to run away from me, that I had done some terrible thing and it was so bad we couldn't talk about it, so she just had to leave. But then she explained that she didn't just want to run away from me, but she even wanted to run away from her own self. Our room, dark and quiet, was the best place to run and hide...and cry. All I had to do was go in once in awhile and give her some reassuring hugs, kisses, and the occasional flowers. (And if I didn't do this? You guessed it; she somehow stored up her emotions for use later on.) It was one of those "Get Well Soon" periods. I got a lot of "man" stuff done during these periods, so we were okay once I convinced her not to run away.

THE CRAMPS

This is what most people consider the typical period. I think it's the only symptom advertisers do commercials on, so maybe it's the most popular kind of period issue. (For you single or newly-married men who think this is all a period is...you are in for a big surprise.) This is the one where Midol and a glass of water did the trick. Then it was like no period at all that month...cool! Except for the extra items at the grocery check-out, that is. But don't forget the Midol, or this period can turn into the bad one. And don't buy the generic stuff. Yeah, I know, I know. It's got the *same* ingredients as the brand name stuff, only it costs a lot less. But SHE doesn't believe that. And don't try to get a brand name bottle and use it over and over again with generic stuff, because she will check the mark on the pill sooner or later. And trust me, you don't need that grief. The buck you save isn't worth it. Get the good stuff, and be thankful it works.

TAKE NO PRISONERS

This is the one I dreaded: "The Period From Hell." And then: "Return of The Period From Hell." And then: "Just Try and Escape From The Period From Hell." You get the picture. The F5 tornado. It lasts only a short time, but destroys anything in its path. This period is like the tornado you might have heard about a few years ago, somewhere in the south. This is the one that even sucked the asphalt off of the streets. This is the one where I was the one crying, "No, No," running away, crying, "Stop, Stop," and hiding and whispering to myself, "Please don't look in here!" There is nothing you can do to stop this force. You gotta run, and you gotta hide.

There are a couple of ways you can get lucky, though. Think about this: have you ever seen those tornados that look like they're just about to slam you, and then they change course, or pull back up in the sky? Sometimes that happens. The trick is to get into one of those submissive postures (as if the alternative of sticking out your chest would make any difference), and maybe, just maybe, it will spare you. This is a helpful maneuver. Second, sometimes you can offer up a sacrifice by doing something you would never,

ever do for her, or buying something you would never, ever buy for her. This doesn't always work, but it is worth a try.

SLEEPY

I got the most done during these periods. The sleepy ones were especially appreciated if they came the month after the "Take No Prisoners" period. I often prayed that I would be left short under the Christmas tree if I could just trade a few of the periods from hell for a few of these periods from heaven.

"Okay," I said to myself. "I think I can handle these periods now, or at least survive them with not too much collateral damage." Every month I had a 4-in-5 chance I would not get my head torn off and have to have it sewn back on again. Of course, periods are like the weather. Sometimes it seems like every storm that hits your house rips out a tree, tears off some shingles, and trashes your yard. But then you get the good runs, where the nice, slow, steady rain on a non-golfing weekend is perfect for your yard and great for an afternoon full of your favorite televised sports.

Chapter 2: The Pre-Hurricane "Periods"

So for my first 10-12 years of marriage, I had got pretty good at figuring out which storm we had this month, making some quick adjustments around the house, and going about my business of being a man, and thankful for it.

Menopause Survival Manual for Men

3

My First Hurricane

Then came something I had never seen or experienced, or even heard about before. It was like living back in the 1600's when weather forecasting was about as refined as brain transplant surgery is today. Now I understand why so many of those ships filled with gold were sunk by storms, never to be found again. They never saw the storm coming, and nobody ever lived to tell about it.

It started out like a "Take No Prisoners" period, but it didn't end as normally scheduled. The shopping part of it did (you know…the tampons, Midol, etc.), but the storm part didn't. Okay, I said to myself, if I am any kind of a man I can hold up through this. But the storm just kept pounding me and pounding me, day after day, and night after night. It started feeling like a half-dozen or more of the worst periods my wife had ever had all bundled up together and feeding upon one another.

After forty days and forty nights (or so it seemed), I cried out to God and said, "Okay, God. I see what they went through in the time of Noah! I see and have experienced first-hand the devastation. Now how about that dove and rainbow?" But it kept coming. And worse, I was used to having just seven days of storm provisions; I was totally unprepared for anything longer. I was horrified at the devastation, but my horror was eclipsed by my dumbfounded-ness. "What in the world *is this*, God?" I asked. I was kind of like those people filming a tornado, in total awe at what they were seeing, but forgetting it is about to mow them down, pick them up, chew them up, and spit them out.

Somehow my wife and I (and our one son still at home) managed to survive this first "different" period, even though it caught us all totally off guard. It wasn't like my wife had watched the weather forecast and forgot to tell me we were getting ready to get slammed by a Category 3.

We lived in California at the time. You know, the land of no tornadoes or hurricanes. We lived in the land of earthquakes. Even though you couldn't predict them, you usually knew within a few seconds if it was going to be a dud, a teaser, a nail-biter, or a "come-to-Jesus" shaker. And we also lived in the land of periods. 7-day periods. Period. So we were left saying to ourselves, "What was that?"

We weren't at the place where humor was helping us yet, though. This was no laughing matter. We were caught totally by surprise. My wife was only 42 at the time, and menopause hadn't entered into our minds yet. We thought it was a "Period Gone Wild," the "Period-From-The-Darkest-Recesses-Of-Hell," or worse yet, some kind of serious illness. So we went to the doctor and were administered a bunch of tests, which all came out negative. Our doctor suggested that it might be early menopause, so we ran those tests, too, but they also came out negative. So we settled for a combination of "Period Gone Wild" and "Period From Hell."

Menopause Survival Manual for Men

4

Clean-up and Rebuild
After the First Hurricane

Clean-up time! Of course, there were hurt feelings and misunderstandings all over the place. We worked on those like we did every other thing that married couples work on.

Except, I just couldn't handle that *"I-just-couldn't-control-myself!"* reasoning my wife gave me. Hey, I can see getting caught off guard once a month for a few hours until the Midol kicks in. But what was up with this? The doctor said it wasn't menopause, and she quit needing feminine products on the right day, so what's the deal? Now I had enough sense by then to know not to open my mouth and say those words, but I was sure thinking them loud!

I mean, come on. Even women know how to exercise some self-control! They do it all the time at the mall when they resist the sale items and go for the new seasonal stuff that isn't on sale. And it really got to me when it seemed like she could hold it together around everyone else but me.

So deep inside I held some resentment.

Like the normal husband with a wife that has "Take No Prisoners" periods, I acted out my resentment instead of speaking it out. The rationale behind this behavior is that we can vent silently without it costing us anything during the next period. (Of course, this is faulty reasoning. Her woman's intuition catches on to it anyway. But you know how we men are...we lie to ourselves thinking it helps anyway.) So I acted out: with my attitude, by not doing things right away when she asked, by conveniently "forgetting" what she had asked me to do, etc. You know, the standard man routine.

And, like I said she would, she caught on. She would ask, "Honey, are you upset at something? Did I say or do something?"

Then came my two responses. The first one was my vocal response: "Of course not, dear, everything is okay. I just had a bad day at..."(fill in the blank). And the second one was what I said silently in my mind: "Gee, dear, what do you think? (*Dear* is what I say when I'm upset.) You cut my head off, stuck your hand down my throat and tore my heart out, and you have to ask if I'm upset at you? Of course I am!"

And when I kept on acting out, then came *her* usual responses: "I don't appreciate your attitude!" or "I don't think I like your tone of voice!"

My turn again. Nothing. My first response is to say nothing. I also tried to look like a puppy dog with his tail between his legs, or maybe like a kid caught with his hand in the cookie jar, or sometimes I just tried to look dumb. I alternated between these looks.

Then I hear that voice in my head: "Well (notice there was no *dear* with this one), I don't like *your* attitude, or the way *you* have been talking to *me* or treating *me* once a month for the last umpteen years, and now it's getting worse! And if I say anything, you blow it off, or act like you can't do anything about it, or act like I'm making too big a deal, or say you do not talk like that to me. Man, I wish I had a tape recorder for last month! And now I make one little peep and you make a big deal about it!"

Whew. That felt as good writing it out as it does every month when I think it in my head, if not better! (I still can't believe I'm actually writing all this, and publishing this for the whole world, and my wife, to see. I'm either insane, stupid, in need of money, very secure in my marriage, or all of the above. My lofty motive is not to help all the suffering men out there, since I don't even know 99.9999% of you! It's probably more that I'm stupid, but need the money. And maybe if I get enough of it, I can give it to my wife, and she will let it slide that I wrote all of this.)

So, I felt bad about the things I wished I could say and about my passive-aggressive behavior. Part of me felt bad just because I knew I had been a jerk. Another part of me felt bad because I wasn't being a jerk when she was on the warpath, but when her guard was down. Sometimes, I knew I had taken advantage of a given situation, and part of me was okay with that—the same part that thought she could control this thing, but just chose not to around me. But as for the other parts of me—the ones that felt she really didn't mean it and that she really does love me—knew I had gone too far. (Whew! Who knew a guy had so many parts?)

So I genuinely apologized, usually with a card and her favorite flowers in hand or close by, hugged her and kissed her, and made up. Both of our feelings got mended, and I started enjoying my heaven-on-earth marriage again.

Menopause Survival Manual for Men

5

What! Another Hurricane?

Just about the time I started to write-off what happened last month as a period out of control, last month came back again. I started to wonder if I was stuck in some kind of twisted time warp or maybe even a "Twilight Zone" re-run that keeps playing over and over again.   Or maybe I was in that movie "Groundhog Day," where the guy had to keep reliving the same day over and over and over again until he got it right.

So the storm hit again, caused the same kind of damage, the same kind of hurt feelings, and the same kind of hidden resentment.

And the same questions arose: "What in the world is going on? I don't live in Florida or Kansas! I live in California. We don't have hurricanes or tornadoes! And besides, a 42-year old woman with good blood test results shouldn't be going through this!" As you can guess, all my kicking and screaming and whining didn't change nature.

We lived in Dana Point at the time, one mile from the ocean, and halfway between Los Angeles and San Diego. Even though the waves were only around 5-8 feet near our house, they still taught me real quick who was boss when I got on my boogie-board. The rip-tides and undertows were vicious, unpredictable, and unforgiving, and the rock-strewn ocean floor made the crashing waves hurt even worse. They could care less about my whining or reasoning. The nickname for these waves are "Killer Dana" waves. If I chose to go into the surf at Dana Point, I had to be prepared not only to have the ride of my life, but get thrashed like I was a sock in a washing machine full of stone, sand, salt, and seaweed. I loved the ride so much that I was willing to pay the price when an occasional wave kicked my butt.

And so it was with this new kind of storm in my heaven-on-earth marriage. I never had any second thoughts about staying in my marriage, but I now had to reckon with paying a new kind of price. Now I didn't have to go to the Dana Point Beach to feel like a sock in a stone-filled washing machine. I could now experience that same raw sensation inside the privacy of my Dana Point home. (And, hey, no sand to clean out of my shorts.) This new kind of storm that was now developing into a regular weather pattern did not care if I didn't "believe" in storms like this during our current stage of life. And it didn't care that there are not "supposed" to be hurricanes in California.

Once I got over the "shock and awe" and my feelings of bewilderment and resentment lessened, my wife and I started talking about this new weather phenomenon in our life. Our weekly walks to the coffee shop and bookstore on Saturday mornings stayed consistent, but I started going to the "Women's Health" section instead of the history or sports sections.

I was looking for books like "The History Of Women in America With Unexplained Long-Lasting Period-Type Symptoms," or "The Period From Hell," or "Periods Gone Wild," or "How to Get Your Butt Kicked by Your Hormonal Wife and Love It." But I found no titles of the sort. There were books on periods, menopause, manic depression, and paranoid schizophrenia set off by mid-life chemical balance changes. (Did they give my wife the blood test for that one?) But I couldn't find one that fit what my wife had and what I was experiencing.

I didn't know where to turn. So reluctantly and desperately, I did the only thing I could think of: I started delving into the dark world of menopause books. After a few Saturday trips to the bookstore, I got a chance to look through enough menopause books to start believing that menopause *must* be what my wife had. Her symptoms sure sounded like what these books described, regardless of what the doctor told us.

So, like any good shade-tree mechanic or Saturday morning home handyman, I started looking for ways that maybe I could help my wife "fix" herself so we could get our life back. I didn't care what the doctor said. I didn't care what the older generation *didn't* say. I was going to help fix this thing, and that's all there was to it. I didn't know how, and I didn't know with what, but I was going to do it. That's what we men do: we FIX things.

Well, it didn't take me long to find out I wasn't going to fix this. And it also didn't take me long to find out that trying to "help" Mother Nature cost me 3 times more than if I had left her alone. I started making a bunch of suggestions based on my readings during our

Saturday trips to the bookstore. "Honey, have you tried this?" Or, "Sweetie, have you considered...?" Maybe even, "Dear (uh-oh, the *dear* word again), can we...?" Barraging your menopausal wife with suggestions on how to "fix" herself is like running your nails down a chalkboard. Of course, I didn't know this at the time, so I kept doing it. That is, until I realized I had to sew my head back on every time I made one of my stupid suggestions.

I discovered quickly that this was going to be harder research than the period books I had read a decade or so ago. At least with the periods, women had started to come up with some answers and were writing about them. But with this menopause thing, they were sure writing about it, but where were the DOGGONE ANSWERS!? I mean, come on, you women have got to be able to figure this thing out! Someone MUST have figured this out! There are around 3 billion women on this planet, and enough of them are going through menopause and having enough hot flashes to cause global warming! (And you thought fluorocarbons are eating up the ozone.) We found a cure for polio and vaccines and antibiotics for almost every disease known to man; surely there has to be a vaccine or antidote for menopause!

But every book I turned to gave me the same grim outlook: "Every woman goes through menopause differently," and "Every woman will have to learn how to work through this." So I started looking through every book, one by one, to see if I could come up with some kind of diagnosis or treatment or concoction for my wife. As I said earlier, we men FIX things! We find out what's wrong, look it up, and fix it! Hey, I mean, we discovered how to track weather patterns and prepare better for storms. We have learned how to construct skyscrapers that endure 7.5 earthquakes, and how to build planes that defy the laws of gravity. We sent a man to the moon, so surely we can figure out the kind of menopause our wives are going through and fix that!

I was kidding myself to think for one minute I could diagnose my wife when she couldn't even figure out how to describe her condition in terms I understood, or even in terms the other women authors were using in the books at the bookstore. If I could have taken pages out of about two dozen of those books, I could almost describe what I *thought* I saw my wife was experiencing. But then, how in the world do you figure out what part of which treatment you take from whose book?

Menopause books started to look to me like diet books. Everyone has this great diet that works for them, and then they publish it and try to sell it to you. I think the way people lose weight is that after buying all the diet books and diet foods and diet pills that are on the market, they are so broke they can't afford to buy any groceries, so they lose weight.

Now I see why so many women opt for the more drastic measures of heavy-duty prescription drugs and/or hysterectomies (and why so many of their husbands gladly fork out the co-payment or non-covered portion for them to do so). But my wife didn't want to go those ways. I can't say I blamed her. As I said in the beginning of this book, she is a vibrant, passionate, humorous woman. She did not want to lose that part of her, and I didn't want to lose that part of her either. That's what attracted me to her so much. I can also see why so many couples get divorced during these dark periods. It takes some real love and commitment to ride this out.

I loved my wife. I married her for better or for worse, in sickness and in health. I defined my commitment as "dedication without an alternative." I figured if God made marriage to be for a lifetime, and He knew in advance about menopause when He made marriage for a lifetime (which He did know…that's the whole "omniscient" thing), that He also must have made me so I could survive this. I just had to figure out how.

6

What Hurricanes Are
Really Made Of

"I can make it through this. I can." I just had to figure out some survival strategies and tactics, like I had with monthly periods. I had to re-work my contingencies.

So the first thing I did was to start categorizing her "menopausal hurricanes" like I had her "periodic tornadoes." As I did this, I recognized that the menopausal hurricanes contained a lot of the same characteristics as the periods; it's just that they came in combinations. Most of the time, the worst hurricanes came more often, and all of the time they hit harder and lasted longer. So I decided to use the national hurricane rating system to explain what I experienced.

The National Weather Service uses the Saffir-Simpson Hurricane Scale to estimate the potential damage a hurricane can cause due to rain, wind damage and flooding.

Saffir-Simpson Hurricane Scale

Category 1	Winds: 64-82 mph Storm Surge: 4-5 feet above normal
No real damage to building structures; damage to unanchored mobile homes; damage to shrubs and trees; damage to poorly constructed signs; some coastal flooding.	
Category 2	Winds: 96-110 mph Storm Surge: 6-8 feet above normal
Some damage to roofing material and windows; considerable damage to mobile homes; some trees blown down; considerable damage to poorly constructed signs; low-lying escape routes flooded 2-4 hrs before hurricane arrival.	
Category 3	Winds: 111-130 mph Storm Surge: 9-12 feet above normal
Some structural damage to small residences; mobile homes destroyed; some large trees blown down; poorly constructed signs destroyed; low-lying escape routes flooded 3-5 hours before hurricane arrival; some terrain flooded up to 8 miles inland.	
Category 4	Winds: 131-155 mph Storm Surge: 13-18 feet above normal
Some complete roof structures destroyed; many shrubs, trees, and all signs blown down; extensive damage to doors and windows; complete destruction of mobile homes; low-lying escape routes cut off 3-5 hours before hurricane arrival; major damage to lower floors of structures near the shore; potential massive flooding up to 6 miles inland.	

Category 5	Winds: greater than 155 mph Storm Surge: greater than 18 feet above normal
Complete roof failure on many buildings; some complete building failures; all shrubs, trees, and signs blown down; complete annihilation of mobile homes; severe damage to windows and doors; extensive damage to lower floors of structures less than 15 feet above sea level; massive evacuation 5-10 miles inland.	

* Find additional information from the National Weather Service at http://www.nhc.noaa.gov/aboutsshs.shtml.

As you can see from the scale, each hurricane contains a combination of events – rain, wind, and flooding – that cause an increasing amount of damage as these three characteristics increase in volume, speed, and intensity (and all the categories are unkind to mobile homes). I have found it to be the same with menopause. The other thing the scale does not mention, but is a commonly-known fact about hurricanes, is that they start out much like any old rain storm with high tides, but they then grow in ferocity as they bear down on you.

The first signs that a menopausal storm was approaching me were my wife's hot flashes and night sweats. I didn't see these symptoms when she just had periods. Now I have a theory about these two events. I think that with a period, a woman's body discharges an egg, loses some tissue, and then rebuilds, which takes a lot of energy. With my wife's menopause, if she didn't have a period, I propose her body was still working as if she should still be having one. So all that energy has to go somewhere, right? So my unscientific explanation was that the energy went into hot flashes and night sweats.

Remember when your wife was pregnant, and she was always hot, but you were always cold because she kept the thermostat down and kicked the covers off? That's kinda what's happening here, except there's no baby to look forward to. I would wake up in the middle of the night, freezing my tail off and soaking wet. I would say to myself, *What in the world was that? Did I piss all over myself or something?* Nope. No smell of urine here. I was half-wet, uncovered, and freezing. And the thermostat was turned down so far that milk would keep fresh.

The next day when I would ask her what had happened, she told me she wakes up in the middle of the night hot, sweating, and her heart about to pound out of her chest. She kicks the covers off of her, gets up to cool herself off, wash herself down, get some dry nightwear, and come back to bed. What I don't know (because I am a heavy sleeper) is that she had kicked her covers off on me. Then as I slept under enough covers for Antarctica, I would kick them off in my sleep. But because the thermostat had been turned down, and I was sweating from having so many covers on me (plus her sweat was all over me, too), I started to freeze, which is when I would finally wake up.

After a few nights of this, she had sleep deprivation from waking up with a pounding heart and burning flesh, and I was getting sick with a cold. So this started making her cranky and me lethargic. Now as you have probably already guessed, my wife is quite "spirited", and I am pretty laid back. Sleep deprivation really juiced up her crankiness scale, but it made me even more laid back. Not a good combination.

Then I found out that night sweats aren't just at night, and hot flashes also come during cold days. If you're having sex with your wife, hot and sweaty isn't a bad thing. But hot and sweaty *and* sleepless and sexless is a terrible thing.

Then came the headaches. I don't know if it was the stress she was going through, the sleeplessness, or some hormonal imbalance, but she started getting some very bad headaches. And they got even worse if she hadn't had anything to eat in awhile.

Oh, eating, that's another thing. Her body craved things just like when she was pregnant. She put on a few pounds, noticed it, and knew she needed to get back to walking, or to the gym. But when she worked out, either the hot flashes overheated her or the lack of sleep quickly exhausted her.

So now imagine being sleepless, sexless, hot, sweaty, headachy, hungry, out-of-shape, depressed, frustrated, and misunderstood. Then imagine irritable, cranky, short-tempered, absent-minded, disoriented, and misunderstood. Then, all in one week, you feel like crying, clinging, sleeping, running, hiding, and hurting (someone else, that is). Now, pretend you feel like this day after day, with no relief in sight, and no magic bullet, and see how you fare! That's what our menopausal wives feel like.

When you are under that much change and turbulence and hurt, you lash out. It's a natural thing for animals and for people. You lash out at whatever is close to you, or at whatever is the last thing that irritated you, regardless of who they are or how big they are. Anything to stop the torment. And anything in your path is fair game.

The ferocity of the damage you (the husband) see being handed out is in direct proportion to the amount of agony she is going through internally. So the higher this particular hurricane hits on the Saffir-Simpson Hurricane Scale, the worse she feels inside.

Unlike the periods, there wasn't an easy answer on how to weather these different categories of hurricanes. The hugs and kisses of the "Crying and Clingy" periods or the "Cry...and Run and Hide" periods didn't work, because the hot flashes meant that I only irritated her when I tried to hug and kiss. Throwing Midol at these storms like throwing a cup of water at a raging forest fire. And unlike the "Take No Prisoners" periods, I couldn't run fast enough, and I couldn't hide well enough for long enough. Similarities to the "Sleepy" periods? There are none!

You may be asking, "Is there any break from this? Don't hurricanes at least have an eye, where you get a little relief?" Read on…

Menopause Survival Manual for Men

7

The "Eye" of the Hurricane

"Eye: what eye?" I have now been in hurricane country for what seems to be a season without end. And unlike our climatological counterpart, there has been no "eye" in these hurricanes, only brief pauses, if you can call them that.

I am not talking about the kind of pause you get when you take a breath as you are blowing up a balloon. Nor the two-second pauses in between sheets of rain in a thunderstorm. And not even the slight rest your clothes get at the bottom of the drum in the dryer. No, it's more like being pulled in an inner tube behind a speed boat at 60 miles per hour, barely catching your breath between oncoming walls of water.

Well, I guess that's not entirely true. You do get a rest when you are sitting on the john if your bathroom ventilation fan is loud enough. Or when you are at work, that is, depending on how much stress your job gives you. Or maybe you can catch a break when you are in your car...unless you have a cell phone. Then she can reach you anytime on that. And saying you are on another call or your battery is going dead works only so often.

Okay, so I'm exaggerating a little bit.

Well, you do get some reprieve when you sleep. But of course that even depends on how much sleep you need. Remember that feeling in the middle of the night when you get so hot you are about to burn up? (You'd better look again at Chapter 6!) The "hot flash?" Really more like a forest fire. And how about when you wake up in the middle of the night with the chills? Remember why? Yes, the "night sweats." You could have waked up as she got out of bed to tinkle for the fourth time. And finally, it could just be a bad dream. *Her* bad dream. A dream bad enough to cause her to cry in her sleep, in which case, you went to comfort her, but she snapped at you even in her sleep because you made her hot flash/nightmare combination even hotter when you tried to hold her. Or, the dream may have waked her up, in which case, she may have punched you because in the dream you left her for someone who didn't keep you up at night. It's a figment of her imagination, of course, but real enough to her to cause a bruise on your arm or leg the next morning.

Now even though *she* had the dream, you still get blamed for it. You must have done something somewhere for that kind of dream to enter her mind. Of course, it has nothing to do with all the smuck on TV these days about middle-age guys having affairs with younger, non-menopausal women. Of course not.

So now, not only have you been awakened a number of times during the night, but she is now mad at you in the morning, and you probably have a cold from freezing half-to-death for the ump-teenth night in a row because the air conditioner is running full-blast!

And that's just menopause with no relief in sight at night! Then there is daytime and weekends! Work becomes a vacation instead of an obligation, and weekend chores are a welcomed way of blowing off some steam. Only don't let your neighbors see you torturing dead rodents or insects, or beating the junk in your garage to a pulp to take out your frustration. Shut the garage door before you do that.

If you are not a little discouraged or depressed with all I've said, you are not human, or else you are very lucky. Maybe you are some super-husband from another planet that has enough mo-jo not to let this stuff phase you, or perhaps you are one of those male-chauvinist guys who bullies his way through his marriage. You might even be one of the lucky lottery winners. Yes, a few women do get to skip menopause, or they only get a light dose of it. Maybe you got the winning "My wife gets to miss menopause" lottery ticket. If you did, I suggest that you shut up and not tell anyone, and tell your wife and kids not to say anything either. Telling people that your wife didn't go through menopause is not a smart move if you want to keep friends. This is because with this lottery ticket, there is no way you can share the prize with anyone, even if you want to. So celebrate your winning ticket in the privacy of your own home with only your wife and kids. Be like the guy who wins $100 million in the "Super Lotto" but stays anonymous, and still keeps his $10/hour job and his mobile home.

Chapter 7: The "Eye" of the Hurricane

So if your wife skipped menopause, you must act around your friends as if she didn't. Memorize the parts of this book that describe the ravaging effects you are not experiencing, and change them just a bit so no one will realize that you just used my story! (I give you permission as long as you don't try to sell it!) And make sure your wife and kids stories are the same as yours.

OK, back to the guys with menopausal wives. If you are discouraged, you may also be tempted to throw in the towel. You know, thousands of husbands do that every year. They just can't take it. Maybe they bought the *Leave it to Beaver* version of marriage, and thought it would be all bliss. They are blissfully ignorant. Maybe they just don't believe this is nature's way of paying the men back because women have to push a baby's 20-centimeter head through a 10-centimeter birth canal and they don't. Or maybe they just decided it's better to hang on to a woman during her prime and *then* move on to a woman young enough to be their daughter when menopause arrives.

I need to let you know that I made a big assumption when I wrote this book. I assumed that those who read it WANT to hold on to their marriages. That they believe in the whole "in sickness and in health, for better or for worse" thing they vowed at their wedding. (What? No one told you that "worse" thing was secret code for menopause? Hey, no one told me either.) I know up to this point I have painted a pretty gloomy picture. But just hang in there with me; there is hope.

As I write this chapter, I would guess my wife is at her worst point in her battle with menopause. At least the worst so far. I mean, how could it get any worse? She's got all the night issues I've talked about in this chapter, plus all the "period stuff" I talked about in the first chapter, and it's all going on at once.

But I also see the wonder in my wife as she continues to grow in wisdom, and seasoning, and humor. I see how much she loves our grandkids. I see how much she loves to go into the city and help the less fortunate. I see how much she wants to be better, especially when she rolls over and snuggles with me every morning, even though she is sometimes chopping my head off a few hours later.

I KNOW this storm can't last forever. I see older couples that have been married for

30-35 years or more, and I see how much they love each other, and how much they are really becoming like one another, where one can finish any sentence the other starts. I want that level of depth. And you can never get it via the "shortcut" route, by bouncing from one young chick to the next. Sure, you might miss menopause. But you also miss what's on the other side.

One of the most beautiful places on earth is Hawaii. Did you know the beauty of that island was born as a result of violent volcanic eruptions? I am convinced by what I see in older people that the other side of menopause can be every much as beautiful…if you can just stay clear of the hot lava, that is.

Menopause Survival Manual for Men

8

Hurricane Warning

Okay, I'm back trying to devise a plan for weathering out these life-storms that are upon us. And once again, the National Weather Service (NWS) has come through for us. Their website offers a plethora of advice concerning what to do if you live in hurricane country when hurricane season approaches, and then what to do if a hurricane is eminent.

In the southeast corner of the United States, the NWS writes that hurricane season lasts from approximately June-July to November-December. Every year the National Weather Service estimates the number of tropical storms at usually no more than a couple dozen and the number of these turning into actual hurricanes at less than half of that. Before sophisticated radar technology was developed, someone had to be on watch 24/7 just to try to guess what might happen. Now they have early warning systems in place so residents usually have a few days to board up their windows, secure their valuables, and head for higher ground.

However, to my knowledge, no one has invented Doppler radar, satellite imagery, aircraft reconnaissance, or other early warning symptoms for menopausal hurricanes.

They strike without warning. Barometric pressures can be lower than ever recorded and wind speeds can exceed anything registered before. They could die down to a tropical storm in 5 minutes, or they could last for days. They can blow you around a little, or rip your house right off its foundation. You never know how fierce the storm will be until it hits. Plus, you don't get a 6-month reprieve between menopause seasons like you do with hurricane seasons, nor, as I pointed out earlier, do you even get an "eye" in a menopausal storm.

So how does a man prepare for a menopausal outbreak of worse-than-hurricane proportions?

There are two types of men about to face yet another hurricane season, just like there are two types of men about to face yet another onslaught of menopause. You've seen the stories on the news. First, you have the man who won't give up. It could be the old, salty guy who's ridden out 40 years of hurricanes. He's the one who weathered through storms before radar and early warning systems, and who thinks you're a wimp if you can't handle that kind of pressure. Or it could be the mellow, white-haired gentleman who stays put because he just loves the home where his ancestors have lived for centuries. But regardless of which one you talk to, their responses to hurricanes are the same:

"Board it up."
"Weather it out."
"Build it back."

Mental toughness, unconditional love, unwavering commitment, insanity, or a combination of the four, keeps them right where they are.

The second type of man gets hit with his first or second hurricane, and packs it up. This kind of life isn't for him. He would rather start over again in another place.

Men are like this when faced with the regular onslaught of menopause. There are men who can't hang with it, and decide to pack it up. And then there are the men like me, and I hope like you, who are either too stubborn to leave or else love our wives too much to leave, or who are some combination of the two. We would rather get our butts kicked a couple times every season and then rebuild, than give in or give up. Our mantra is the same as the un-budging hurricane veterans:

> *"Board it up."*
> *"Weather it out."*
> *"Build it back."*

Let's look at how we can apply these techniques from the hurricane vets to our situation.

Board (and Sandbag) It Up
 This is hurricane terminology for boarding up anything that can break and for bagging anything that can get wet. You do all you can to minimize the damage. You raid your garage for every board and nail you can find, and then join the throngs at the home improvement stores and eat up the lumber section like a swarm of locusts. Then you find any bag you can (burlap preferably, but pillow cases, tied-up shirts, and sleeping bags will

work, too), and fill it, preferably with sand, to wall out the water. And you do all this, knowing deep in your gut that it may or may not work. Chances are that things are still gonna break, and things are still gonna get wet.

If you have sensitive feelings, or your temper gets easily ruffled, you better figure out a way to deal with that rather quickly. Hurricanes do not have consciences. They don't feel remorse. Hurricanes aren't considerate. They don't care how you feel, or if you have had a bad day at work. Hurricanes don't have good timing. They don't care if you're down to your last nerve. And they don't care if you just painted your house, just planted new shrubs, or just put on a new roof.

You can't take it personally. If you do, you're beat. It's the same way with menopausal hurricanes.

Your wife doesn't mean to tear your heart out and stick it in the garbage disposal. She doesn't mean to be totally insensitive to you, while expecting you to be able to read her mind and feelings, even though she knows you can't read her mind and has told you countless times before she knows you can't, and never will, because you're are a man, and it's okay. But now it's suddenly *not* okay. The hormonal wind speeds and tidal surges inside of her don't know any other way to relieve the lowest barometric pressures ever measured. The lower the pressure, the worse the hurricane's destruction.

So just board it up and bag it up.

And prepare yourself to be mistreated and misunderstood, and more importantly, be prepared to be okay about it. Just keep telling yourself she can't help it; she doesn't know what she is doing. Watch an old werewolf movie. Pay close attention to the uncontrollable urges, the violent temper, and then the loss of memory and the remorse. That's what she is going through. That will give you a little sympathy and insight.

Weather it Out

Once you have boarded and bagged it up, you need to have a game plan to save your life when the storm hits. If you can find and make higher ground, do it. Higher ground can take on many different forms when a menopausal hurricane hits. You have to use every bit of ingenuity and cunning you can muster up.

It may be longer-than-normal restroom visits (a sudden, unexplained case of the runs works every once in a while). Or, it may be spending more time with the kids helping them with homework (even if you know nothing about the subject they are taking...bribe them to play along). Then there is always overtime at work, or those home improvement projects you have been dreading that now look like a tropical vacation.

If you can't run and hide, then you need to find some ways to blow off some of your temper and hurt feelings in a constructive way. Use hand tools instead of power tools for your next home improvement project. Rollerblade that 10-mile commute to work. Or cut your grass with scissors. And if you can't find anything constructive to do, go vent your pent-up feelings on a grizzly bear. Do anything. But don't lash back at your wife. It won't work any better than you trying to stop the onslaught of a 10-megaton hurricane by holding up your hand and yelling, "Stop!"

What if you can't escape or you can't find any grizzlies to wrestle? What if...you have to spend time with your wife when her winds are hitting 150 mph? A full answer to this question follows in Chapter 11, but my emergency tip? Be nice, be agreeable, be co-operative, be apologetic, etc. And, you can always do what the old nuclear attack posters told us to do when we were in grade school: "Get on the floor, put your head between your legs, and kiss your ass goodbye!"

Build it Back

Once the storm is over, you have to survey the damage and do repairs. If you don't, the next storm will rip your home to shreds. You may be tired from weathering the storm, but now's not the time to rest. Now's not the time to feel sorry for yourself and mope for days or weeks, lamenting the damage to or loss of your home and your hard work. Now's the time to rebuild and to fortify your castle, because trust me, another storm is coming sooner than you think.

Your wife is in one of those rare moments of sanity when you can actually express how YOU feel and still walk away with your head intact. You need to share with her constructively, and try to get some hints at how you can handle the storm better next time. The nice thing about menopausal women, as opposed to catastrophic hurricanes, is that the woman will usually tell you how it felt to be menopausal. A hurricane will not. So benefit from this slight technical advantage. Find out how she feels, how she thinks, and what she feels and thinks about how *you* reacted to the storm.

And take good notes.

You also need to build some good feelings between each other and have some good times with each other during this brief lull in the storm. This is another thing you have going for you with a menopausal woman that you don't with a menopausal weather system. Goodwill actually pays off a little. You need every "little" you can get.

You won't feel like doing this because your nerves and feelings will have been shredded. But you have to push through and do it.

Convince yourself that the woman you are now with is the same, sweet, sexy lady you married *X* years ago. (She really is deep inside, you know). Treat her like she has never hurt you or been mean to you. Don't treat her like she has treated you recently, but treat her like she has treated you in the sweetest times of your marriage. You have to pull out the Golden Rule on this one: Love her like you want her to love you.

There will come a time later on into hurricane season for you to express your hurts and feelings. But please trust me: hold off a few more chapters before you attempt this, or you could get knocked back into the Stone Age.

9

Attempts to Neutralize Hurricanes

Man has always been driven to try to conquer or control anything in his way, including hurricanes. The website of the Hurricane Research Division of the Atlantic Oceanographic and Meteorological Laboratory (AOML) responds to questions about what we are doing to stop these monster storms. Take a look at the "Frequently Asked Questions" section. I have shortened the questions and answers a little, as well as weeding out the scientific stuff that I don't even pretend to understand, but this is what I found—honest!

1.   *Why don't we try to destroy hurricanes by seeding them with some kind of chemical?*
       Actually, for a couple of decades we tried to do just that. But what we thought were our early successes, which encouraged us to keep trying, were actually found to be natural

changes in some storms that caused them to weaken all on their own.

2.   *Why don't we try to destroy them by placing a substance on the ocean surface that would prevent evaporation from occurring, so not as much moisture gets sucked up into the hurricane?*

There was some experimental work done in this area, too. If it would work, the storms would quickly weaken, because they need water to maintain their intensity. However, finding a substance that would be able to stay together in the rough seas of a hurricane proved to be the downfall of this idea.

3.   *Why don't we try to destroy them by adding some kind of water absorbing substance to the storm itself?*

We experimented with a substance called "Dyn-O-Gel," which absorbs large amounts of moisture and then becomes a gooey gel. It was proposed that we drop large amounts of the substance into the clouds of a hurricane. We weren't able to draw any conclusive results because of logistical problems. We would need so much of the experimental substance that it would take six C-5A heavy-lift transport airplanes flying into or over the hurricane every minute! (MY question is, where in the world do you store that much Dyn-O-Gel?)

4.   *Why don't we just nuke 'em?*
        You would have to blow up a 10-megaton nuclear bomb every 20 minutes to equal the force of an average hurricane. Or, to look at it another way…according to the 1993 *World Almanac*, in the year 1990, the entire human race used electricity at a 20% lower rate than the power of one average hurricane! And even if you tried to "nuke" it, the environmental and health fallout would be worse than the hurricane itself. Their conclusion: "Brute force interference with hurricanes doesn't seem promising."

5.   *Why don't we try and destroy them by other means?*
        We have considered numerous other methods over the years to modify hurricanes: cooling the ocean with icebergs, blowing the storm away with windmills. (You've GOT to be kidding!)

But as carefully reasoned as some of these "suggestions" are, they all share the same shortcomings: they fail to appreciate the size and power of a hurricane.

In closing, the website states:

"If the time comes that men and women can travel at nearly the speed of light, we will figure out a way to come up with enough brute-force intervention in hurricane dynamics...Perhaps the best solution is not to try to alter or destroy [them]. but just to learn to co-exist better with them."

Ah, something we can use...

ATTEMPTS TO NEUTRALIZE MENOPAUSE

Man has also made his attempts to neutralize menopause. When my wife was finally clinically diagnosed as having menopause, the first thing they wanted to do was try to "nuke" it. That's my term for the most drastic measure, a hysterectomy. Just take out the parts that they think are causing the problems, throw in some hormone replacement therapy (which is now being shown to be more harmful than beneficial in many cases), and that's that. But there was one big problem: the massive side effects, or to put it in "nuke" terms, the environmental damage. If you haven't heard it yet, a lot of women that go through a hysterectomy are never themselves again. Kind of like a "gynecological lobotomy" from what I understand. That's not what I want for my wife. I would rather deal with the ravages of hurricanes and get to the other side one day, seeing glimpses of her old self along the way, than to have the peace of a subverted menopause, but the emptiness of losing forever the parts I love most about my wife.

Then there are man's attempts to use pharmaceutical equivalents of "Dyn-O-Gel" on it to "goo" it. I guess the best equivalent to this would be to treat the psychological effects of menopause with drugs. My wife looked at this option, but too often the effects "goo" your vibrancy or thought processes. She declined, and I agreed. We didn't want that either.

Finally, there are attempts to "cloud seed." This example utilizes hormone therapy without a hysterectomy and without anything like "Dyn-O-Gel." My wife is still experimenting with these. (It also seems like someone is coming up with some "new" concoction every few months, which makes finding the one that might work even more elusive.) Some have helped, and others haven't. After two years, she is still trying to find the right mix of the right things for her. But just when she thinks she has things under control, her system changes on her (and me) again. No silver bullet yet.

Let me make a disclaimer at this point before a doctor reads this and goes ballistic. I am NOT a doctor, and I have NO medical training and NO medical experience. The things I just noted about medical procedures and medications are my wife's and my OPINIONS on these things concerning MY WIFE ONLY, so please take it as just that. We believe that medicine is a "practice," just like the doctors say: "I PRACTICE medicine." Haven't you ever heard your doctor say: "Try this, and let's see how it works, and if not, we'll TRY something else?" Why do you think you are always signing all those disclaimers when you go to the doctor? And why do you think every prescription advertisement on TV or in magazines lists a zillion possible side effects?

My wife and I understand it's OUR responsibility to take the educated, experiential opinions of the doctor, do our own research if we wish, and then make as informed a decision as we can. So what I mentioned above are the decisions we made for ourselves. You have to do your own research and make your own decisions about what you are willing to try. At this point, other than experimenting with a few prescriptions and vitamins, we have opted for exercise and nutrition and prayer.

And, of course, escape routes and storm shelters. And lots of plywood, nails, and sandbags.

I am also trying to put in place the advice the National Weather Service arrived at after decades of experimentation with altering hurricanes: "Perhaps the best solution is not to try to alter or destroy them, but just to learn to co-exist better with them."

Make friends with the hurricane. Or at least start to somehow try and stand up to it. But that can be harder than you think.

For more information, you can visit the Atlantic Oceanographic and Meteorological Laboratory's FAQ website:
http://www.aoml.noaa.gov/hrd/tcfaq/tcfaqHED.html.

Menopause Survival Manual for Men

10

The "Perfect" Storm

After experiencing and analyzing these new types of menopausal storms and after doing all my internet research into real hurricanes, AND after trying to apply this information to my situation, AND AFTER devising some survival plans for weathering them and maybe even some counter-measures for reversing them, it was obvious that my past 12 years' experience in learning how to survive periods, and my rookie-knowledge of hurricanes and menopause were not helping very much. I needed a fresh plan, and I needed it fast. But even if I could have completed my task, what happened next would have ripped through any strategy I had developed for riding it out.

I got hit with the "Perfect Storm."

This was the storm they named a movie after, remember? The actual storm happened in 1990 in the North Atlantic. Okay, if you're like me, you probably remember the movie better than the actual events. This was the movie where George Clooney played deep-sea fisherman, Captain Billy Tyne. He and his buddies got caught in the middle of the convergence of three weather systems, each one a widow-maker in its own right. (If you haven't seen the movie, you need to. It will teach you that there are some storms you don't mess with.) Capt. Tyne had one chance to get away, and he didn't take it. And it cost him everything.

Well, here is the story of *my* perfect storm.

Weather System #1

May, 1998. My dad had just come to live with us. We knew he was pretty bad off, and we decided that until he had to be moved into a nursing home, he would be staying with us. You see, both my wife and I had agreed years before that if my dad or her mom got to where they could not take care of themselves, we would take them in. She was raised by her mom, and I was raised by my dad, and after all they had sacrificed for us, we always knew we would do this for them. So my dad moved in, and we all agreed he could stay as long as he could get himself to the bathroom.

Living with my dad was not easy. He moved in with many ailments and enough medications to fill a shoebox. But to make matters worse, unknown to us, he had been having memory problems and fainting spells, which sometimes caused him to mess up his regular prescription doses. So, when he moved in, he was basically like a strung-out drug addict in withdrawal. He was cranky and demanding, and he stayed awake and was too loud, too late at night, and woke up too loud, too early in the mornings. But he was my dad, and I loved him.

Weather System #2

It was June, 1998, one month after my father came to live with us. The company where I had been working for only six months began to show some signs of having its own storm to deal with. Let me give you a little history.

An unsolicited phone call in 1997 had led to an offer of a full-time, senior level position with a non-profit organization half-way across the country. It was something I had always wanted to do, but could never afford to until that time. Accepting that offer meant that I would leave the Fortune 500 company where I had a very promising career, a six-figure income, stock options, and some hefty promotions waiting just over the horizon. (Was I going through menopause to do such a ludicrous thing?) I relocated my family from Ohio to California and started this new career in January, 1998. Now, six months into the new job, I wished I could get my old job back. But of course, it was too late.

So now I was stuck dealing with my sick dad and while my professional career grow more and more uncertain. Could it get any worse?

Weather System #3

July, 1998, and my wife is miserable. A significant source of this grief was the situation with my dad and with my job. My wife was the one caring for my dad all those hours while I was at work (having given up her own job to do so), and then when I got home each day, she had to walk though all of my job crises with me. Those two things alone would be too much for anyone, but unfortunately, that wasn't all of it. When we moved for me to take my "dream" job, she had given up a job she absolutely loved and a place she had grown to love, for the second time in our marriage.

You see, back in 1989, the company I worked for then had transferred us from California to Ohio. Moving wasn't anything for me because I had done it all my life. But my wife had lived in California all her life, as did all of her family and friends. So this initial move was very hard for her.

When the opportunity arose for us to go back to California in 1998, I thought it would be a dream come true. I naively thought the move back would be a blessing for her. After all, I moved us back to a much nicer place than we had ever lived, almost on the ocean. And we lived very near her brother and sister, whom she had missed so much.

So what did I do wrong here? After living in Ohio for eight years, she had made a new life for herself, and once again, she had to give up everything. And all the wonderful things that I promised this move would bring were taken away because of my dad's illness and the problems on my job. Instead of my being sensitive to her struggles, I was too wrapped up in my own issues to notice how unhappy she was. And the fact that I didn't get it was as much of a problem as her being unhappy in the first place.

Weather Systems Collide

It was now August, 1998. I was still treating these three weather systems as three distinct events, each one needing as much attention as I could give it. Our home was upside down because of my dad, my entire career was in a state of uncertainty because of my job, and my heaven-on-earth marriage was strained because of how our move affected my wife. And remember, all three crises had boiled up to the surface in the space of three very short months.

But I actually thought I was making progress on all three fronts. Now that I look back, I guess part of that confidence came from the fact that I am an optimistic person at heart. Secondly, I had confidence in my perceived ability to "fix" things, to figure out how to get my hands around the issues and work them through for everyone's benefit. And I am now sure that the third reason for my confidence is that I am as naturally perceptive as a rock.

I adjusted my work schedule to spend more time at home helping with my dad. I also made some changes at work, not only to compensate for needing to be home more, but also to weather some of the problems the company was having. And I tried to get my wife away from all the chaos more often.

But then came something I did not anticipate: not only did each storm grow stronger, but they started to converge to form one huge "super-storm" that would try to tear everything apart.

The Perfect Storm Arrives...

Wave #1:   We found out that my dad's lung cancer was inoperable, and he had maybe three months to live. He started inviting all kinds of friends and family over without considering the pressure it put us under, especially my wife, who was home with my dad while I worked all week.

Wave #2:   The wheels started to come off of the organization I had uprooted my family for. I became so pre-occupied my own career crisis that I was not paying attention to my wife and her needs.

Wave #3: My wife couldn't handle the pressure. She told me she wanted to leave. This wasn't the "leave" of the run, cry, and hide periods. This was the real thing. Not leave me, but leave period, and not knowing where to go. The combined effect of my dad's illness, our cross-country move, and a menopause that neither of us fully understood was enough to make anyone want to escape the onslaught.

So, within the space of a few weeks, I was faced with the prospect of no dad, no job, and no wife.

I know this chapter isn't funny...sorry. But for those of you who are reading this book because you are going through a menopausal hurricane, I know you appreciate the grueling honesty of this chapter. It puts us in this thing together, and we need all the "together" we can get.

So here I am, in the roughest time of my professional life, with the full weight of a mid-life crisis looming over me like a dark cloud. I am questioning my decisions, my professional future, and my purpose for the last half of my life.

I have once again uprooted my wife from friends, family, and a job she loved as much as any she had ever had. She is going through her own mid-life crisis, as well as a transitional crisis that I am responsible for.

And my dad is dying.

And to top it all off, we have a menopausal nightmare that has proved itself capable—all by itself—to wreak havoc on our lives without any other crisis going on. But now, with these other things thrown in, together they have served as ingredients to elevate the intensity of everything we are going through to the point of being unbearable.

And to top all THAT off, I didn't feel I could say anything. I was hurting, but the atmosphere was so fragile that I felt like one errant word would bring everything that was left crashing down. So I just ate it and tried to hold the pieces together as best as I could.

The problem is that things I thought wouldn't matter, mattered. And the things I thought *would* matter didn't. I did not know how to get out of this. Looking back to the movie, I felt like Capt. Billy Tyne when he tried to turn the boat away from the storm, only to find that the storm was raging there, too. And when a glimmer of light peeked through the clouds, the surrounding darkness choked it out.

What I couldn't see or understand at the time is that my wife felt the same way I did. I couldn't see it because I was taking her shots personally. Somehow, everything got turned around, like when you are trying to save someone who is drowning, only she thinks you are trying to drown her. The drowning person cannot see you as her savior, but instead, sees you as her enemy. My wife couldn't see that I was trying to help her, and I couldn't see that she was not just mad at me.

This dark season in our marriage allowed me to see why so many marriages are ruined a result of menopause. But I chose not to take the only way out of my perfect storm.

I'm glad I made the choice I did.

11

Facing Down the Hurricane

Up until this point, we have proceeded on an assumption based on an old saying: "Even a live dog is better than a dead lion." This is the strategy I chose to use during the "perfect storm" of the last chapter. I chose my words and actions very carefully, tip-toeing as much as I could to keep from upsetting the fragile state of affairs our life was in.

But there is some weird thing that happens with these "human hormonal hurricanes" that does not apply to its climatological counterpart. As time goes by, the human strain of these storms somehow senses fear, and gradually starts to feed off of it to gain even more strength and ferocity.

I haven't figured out if the fear unleashes pent up energy in my wife for all the times I said or silently proclaimed "I'm the boss," or raised my voice asserting my "manly" rights. Or the times I forgot to bring home flowers the day after an argument, or forgot yet another anniversary, or Valentine's Day (which I did just this year, knuckle-headed me) and had to make up a tall one like: "I left the card at work," or "I did a nice card on the internet but a virus ate it," (the 21st-century-version of *The dog ate my homework*). But for some reason, as more time went by trying to appease the hurricane with fear-motivated acts of self-preservation, the more the hurricanes grew in their ferocity. It took me a while to figure this out. But once I did (which started to happen towards the end of our "perfect storm"), I decided that sometimes a man just has to take a stand.

Men are not built to just "take it" all of the time. We are not constructed to run and hide. Even from a hurricane. Every once in awhile you will hear about the guy who faced down the hurricane and rode out the storm. I am not talking about the occasional moron who didn't know any better, or the drunken fool who didn't even know there was a hurricane.

I am referring to the guy who knows what's in store for him and just doesn't care anymore what it costs him. This is the man who has tried everything to minimize the storms' damage to his home, all to no avail. He has boarded everything up, each year with thicker boards and longer nails. His roof shingles are so thick they would protect the space shuttle during re-entry. He has weighted his sandbags with lead, and secured his trees better than skyscrapers. Yet the storm still finds a weakness in his work, a chink in his armor. And once it finds an opening, all hell rushes in and blows his house up from the inside out. This is the man who is tired of the beating, but also refuses to move away. This is his land and his house and his life, and he is going to hold on to what is his, or die trying.

And this is EXACTLY how I was feeling. I felt I had tried everything to appease the indiscriminate wrath of menopause, with only minimal effect, if any. I was tired of the beating. This was my life, and my wife, and my family, and I wasn't going to leave any of it. I am going to hold onto what is mine, or I am going to die trying.

The man who finally stands up to the hurricane makes his usual preparations for the oncoming storm, only this time, he waits patiently for its arrival instead of running to higher ground. Then the storm hits. Every time the storm tries to knock off a board, he is right there to nail it back on. If a sandbag tries to move, he has more lead to throw on it. If a shingle starts to tear, he lashes himself to the house (like Captain Ahab lashed himself to the whale in *Moby Dick*) and fixes it. And when the storm gets too strong to venture outside, he beats back every bullet of water and spear of wind with boards, nails, sandbags, furniture, and anything he can get his hands on.

Then, finally, the storm stops. The man exits from his fortress tired and bruised, but alive. The roof is missing some shingles, but unlike past storms, the roof itself is not missing. His house looks like it has been sandblasted, but it is still his house. Some sandbags have moved, but the ones inside plugged most of their holes. The wood over the windows is splintered, but not torn off. The inside is wet, but not flooded up to the second story.

Now I have decided to be that man, albeit in a different type of storm: a storm of mega-menopausal proportions.

Here is my story of finally deciding to face down the storm.

Chapter 11: Facing Down the Hurricane

First, I decided I would believe that the storm can exert some self-control (unlike its climatological counterpart), even though it doesn't believe it can. I started noticing some chinks in the storms' armor. How could my wife, in the midst of a Category 5, suddenly become calm? At first I thought it was just the eye of the hurricane, but then I started noticing a pattern of calm versus storm. The calm would come more often around non-family members, and the storm more often around family.

So I tried to come up with a game plan for having this kind of conversation with my wife. I knew I needed some serious brownie points to even stand a chance. So, over the next few weeks, I did all the things a husband would do to make his wife feel special, say, on her birthday. And I did that every day for a few weeks, until she quit asking what I was up to.

Then one day, when I felt I had built up enough points, and I had built up enough courage, and I had her off-guard, I struck.

I started the "co-exist with the hurricane" strategy that the National Weather Service had suggested. I spoke in such a way as I never thought I would humble myself to speak. I started talking about "my feelings." I quit trying to use "male reasoning" and started sharing how I "felt" when the storms would hit. How do you know what words to use here? You have to think back on how your wife shares her feelings with you and the words she uses when she talks…you know, words like "valued," "loved," "cared for," "protected," or "secure." Or words that are the opposite of these. And if you still don't have your vocabulary loaded up enough, rent some chick flicks, or start browsing through the women's magazines at the grocery store or the unisex barber shop you go to. (But make sure you get an older, male barber, and not a female one, and then explain to him *why* you are reading women's magazines. He will understand.)

I pointed out to my wife that smack in between the tremendous storm surges around me was this unexplainable calm around other people. And that this had not just happened once, but on a number of occasions.

Let me pause for a moment. You may be wondering why you couldn't have just skipped to this chapter of the book to begin with. There is a good answer. These little tips I have just shared with you only work at the right time and place in the hurricane season. Use them at the wrong time and the storm will ravage you even more. Only with experience weathering some storms can you gain the wisdom to know when to stand up to a storm and how to go about doing it.

Also, some weird phenomenon occurs with these storms: it's almost as if they gain respect for you once you have let them shred you time after time. You keep hanging in there; you don't run, and you don't try to nuke them. Then the storm *almost* (I said "almost!") starts to feel sorry for you, and is willing to "let" you pay homage to it by sharing your feelings. Maybe the storm figures it has really beaten you when you, as a man, humble yourself to the point you are actually sharing "feelings."

Okay, let's go on. So you share your "feelings," and let her know that you are hurting, too. And you share with her how you have been hurt. You appeal to the deepest part of any woman. In fact, this is the same part of her that is getting beat up by a menopausal hurricane, too. And now that you have been ravaged by these storms just as she has, you have built up enough goodwill for her to even want to hear about your feelings.

I guess it's the old "misery-loves-company" thing.

You are now in one of those rare moments that most straight men never experience. You are in the middle of an emotional moment with a woman, seeing eye-to-eye and heart-to-heart.

You should now hear her say things like:
"Gee, honey, I didn't know I was doing that," or
"Gee, honey, I hurt you like that?"
"Gee, honey, I didn't know you felt like that," or
"Gee, honey, let me think about that."

If you are not getting these kinds of replies, you need to go back and weather a few more storms in order to experience this greater transformation into a man who can see eye-to-eye and heart-to-heart with his wife. Remember, a woman can sense when you are sincere, or you are just saying these things because you think it will "fix" things. This is why you need to GO through (not just READ through) Chapters 1-10 before you even *think* about using these tactics. If you try to cheat on this one, she will sense your insincerity sooner, not later, and then you're REALLY in for it! Some things you just don't do…you don't tug on Superman's cape, you don't spit into the wind, you don't pull the mask of the old Lone Ranger, and you *don't* mess with a menopausal female!

But…if you DO hear these kinds of words, then don't take advantage of this rare moment to get back at her for hurting you. That will backfire. Instead, help her learn how to recognize how she is hurting you and what will help so she doesn't keep hurting you. Also, ask her what you can do to help her.

As you go through this period, remind yourself: *"The storm is my friend…the storm is my friend…the storm is my friend."* Don't show fear, and don't exhibit anger.

And give her some time and space to process what she has just heard from you. She, as is the custom for almost all women, will ponder what you have said for days. She will absorb it into the very fabric of her being. And she will (dare I say, *should*?) eventually start treating you more like a fellow human being with a heart and with feelings, rather than the roof shingles, windows, or shrubs you have felt like for Lord-knows-how-long.

Menopause Survival Manual for Men

12

When Hurricane Season
Is Finally Over

Then one day, the storms stopped.

At least I *think* they did.

I *hoped* they did!

It had been hurricane season at my home for nearing 6 years. I had become accustomed to them. I had learned how to get beat up by them. I had learned how to weather them. I had even learned how to stare them down, look them straight in the eye, and stand up to them. I had become a white-haired, storm-hardened veteran. I was a man in the midst of constant battles for his life, who lived through every one of them to tell about it (and write about it). I had even made friends with them.

I had become so used to the storms that I felt either suspicious or lost without them. The suspicious part was that when a month passed without a storm, it usually meant she was gearing up for a big one. This suspicion was justified, because that's usually how it worked.

Then one month became two months, and then three, and still no new hurricane. We still had occasional tropical storms, but nothing like what the storms used to be. The suspicion turned to a sense of being lost. I was like a fully-armed soldier with no war to fight. I didn't want to let down my guard, but I also wanted to get on with my life. I was in this weird no-man's land. I was a man-on-pause once again, but this was a new kind of pause.

My wife was slowly starting to return to parts of her normal self. The sunrises and sunsets didn't always have storm clouds covering them. There were actually a few that were as beautiful as ever. The beaches were beginning to come back, and the sand was even white in places. The lemonade on the front porch didn't always have ice in it, but at least we were back on the porch. Even the flowers were returning. But was Mother

Chapter 12: Hurricane Season is Finally Over

Nature playing some cruel trick on me, lulling me into some kind of false sense of security? Or was it really over? I remember hearing some stories from elderly couples about how the later years of their marriage were even better than the earlier years (I am sure they meant the "pre-menopause" years). Was I getting ready to experience this myself? Were my wife and I getting ready to enter into the best years of our lives, the time that makes it all worth it?

I hope so.

A few months later…I *think* we are.

Later still…This *has* to be it!

Am I dreaming? Oh, just pinch me!

If I had waited any longer to finish this book, countless men would still be suffering needlessly. But for the sake of you other poor souls out there, let's assume that this 12-month reprieve is the real thing. I've never had more than a 12-day reprieve before, so I think this is it! (NOTE: My wife is still suffering from some of the effects of menopause, such as fatigue, some night sweats, some sleeplessness, and still trying to keep off a few pounds. But these symptoms are like a gentle rain on a mild spring day compared to what we have been through!)

Life is starting to get good again. We are more experienced, seasoned, and wiser. We are enjoying our three kids and our three grandkids in a way we have not experienced together in a long time (actually, never with the grandkids, because none of them were born before hurricane season). Petty disagreements and little everyday things no longer seed a cloud that is already ready to burst and drown us. The heart-to-heart empathy is now a part of who I am, but I can also actually "reason" some with my wife when she gets upset...and she listens to me! Then I look over my shoulder, waiting for the repercussions...and none come! Quiet is no longer just the eye of the storm. The bathroom is the bathroom once again and not a storm shelter.

We have a new respect and a deeper love for one another than ever before. We have a seasoned wisdom that others notice and are drawn to. We think more alike and finish each other's sentences better. And the amazing thing is that we are doing all these things in our late 40's and early 50's and not in our 60's or 70's! Amazing because most of us think that's how long we have to wait to get to this point. Too many men don't think this is worth waiting for. They have quit or run away long ago.

I started writing this book in the middle of the second-worst storm I ever weathered (remember when I was laid up after knee surgery and asked for ice one too many times?). I started writing as much for my survival as I did for yours. When I wrote the chapter about how to stand up to the storm, it was more of a "real-time" journal of what I was experiencing then and there, not recollecting what I had considered about from years back. Even just a few paragraphs ago, those hesitant pauses were real.

You have caught the real sights, sounds, and emotions of the moment. You have experienced the raw feelings before they had a chance to callous over or be softened by time.

And now you are getting to experience me after the flowers and trees have started to grow back, and the sand is building back up on the beach.

I was thinking the other day about a huge benefit of being out of hurricane season. I am also out of tornado country! Being on the back side of menopause also means you are on the back side of periods! No more periods! No more Russian roulette, no wondering if this month will be cry, run, or cringe. Not to mention all the money I will save not having to buy those feminine products every month. Actually, I may have spoken too soon, because now I have to pay for a thyroid prescription, vitamins, and a couple of different hormonal creams. But I'm not complaining, because the periods are gone, thank God Almighty, the periods are gone! (I am so excited now about the periods ending because I did not have a chance to celebrate them when they *actually* ended...because menopause started.)

The other thing this means for me, and for all you men who will shortly follow me out of hurricane season and tornado country, is that our accountability has increased. We can no longer use hormonal episodes as reasons for running, hiding, or lashing out. And, after so many years of doing these things, we have developed some survival habits that worked well under storm conditions but fail miserably under normal weather patterns.

If we were forced to live as hermits or soldiers during certain time periods, we have probably become comfortable or conditioned at doing so. We must come to grips with this and make some changes to warfare mentality and come out of hiding. We may have to adjust an attitude that always put us on the defensive as if we expected to be hit with 150 mph winds, 20-foot storm surges, and torrents of rain. But the winds are now balmy and mild, the tide comes lazily in and out, and the rains are gentle. We can't rely on sandbags, plywood, shovels, and nail guns anymore.

We may have to learn how to romance our wives again, instead of running to the foxhole. Romancing our wives again...that sounds good. Only this time, it's sweeter. The motivation is more pure. It's no longer about what we are trying to get, but about what we got. I feel sorry for all the guys that bailed out on their menopausal wives. They will never know the joy and fulfillment we are now experiencing. Oh well, they should have ridden out the storm. You know, even nature teaches us this. Big storms wipe out the good stuff, yes, but all that grows back in even more splendor, because all the bad stuff got washed away, too.

So for all you guys reading this book, again I tell you—hang in there…it's *all* worth it.

APPENDIX

GLOSSARY OF HELPFUL TERMS and PHRASES

Disclaimer for anyone out there who has financial, medical, or other interests in any of these words or phrases: Many of the phrases and terms in this section are the unscientific, sarcastic ramblings of a man driven partially insane by the effects of menopause, and should not be taken to resemble any persons, places, or things, either real or imagined.

Barometric Pressure
One of the conditions that determine which category of hurricane is coming at you. In layman's terms: the ability of the storm to suck out all life in the general vicinity, take the energy from it, and convert it into destructive winds. How do you measure the barometric pressure in a menopausal storm before it hits you? I have no idea. Actually, if I knew that, I would be richer than Bill Gates.

Cramps
The most common side effect of periods (at least, the one most advertised on TV).

101

Downburst

In "weather" terms: a sudden downburst of wind from a severe thunderstorm that can cause just as much damage as a tornado at the point of ground contact. In menopause terms: you thought it was just a regular "rough" period, but all of a sudden, you get knocked on your butt, your clothes torn to shreds, and your remote control broken into microscopic pieces from out of nowhere.

Heart Palpitations

This phrase used to indicate what your wife's chest did when she saw you coming when you were dating her. Now it's what your wife's chest does in the middle of the night when she wakes up in a hot sweat and feels her heart is about ready to come out of her chest.

Hormonal Imbalance

The "catch-all" term used to describe the source (from a medical point-of-view) of all the symptoms and ravages of menopause.

Hot Flash

A sudden dramatic increase in your wife's body temperature. Menopause books will try to explain the cause of these temperature changes. Men don't really care what causes them, only how it affects them at night.

Hurricane Season
Any time after periods stop (or start going wild) until you experience at least a 3-6 month calm.

Hurricane Warning
Hot flashes, night sweats, shorter-than-normal temper, or sudden mood changes.

Hurricane Watch
Any time, and every day thereafter, that you have experienced your first menopausal hurricane.

"I gotta go to the bathroom real bad!"
What you tell your wife when you see you are about to get hit by a huge menopausal wave.

"I need to go the hardware store."
What a man says to another man in the presence of their wives to let the *other* guy know that the tropical storm is starting to turn into a hurricane and the first guy is trying to gear up for it.

Menopause
A.k.a. Hurricanes, "The Change of Life," "Hell on Earth," "Woman's-way-of-getting-back-at-us-for-having-to-birth-our-children," etc.

Mother Of All Periods
A.k.a. "Period From Hell," "Period Gone Wild," etc.

Midol
The only over-the-counter medicine that any man I've ever met knows to get or to ask for at the grocery store when his wife is making his day miserable. The supposed "silver bullet" against PMS.

Night Sweats
Used to be what happened when you made love to your wife on a hot summer night. Now, a term used to describe the after-effects of a menopausal hot flash, and also the reason why you wake up freezing and soaking wet in the middle of the night when you did *not* piss on yourself.

Perfect Storm
When a menopausal storms and other "life" storms are slamming you at the same time or in short succession.

Period

A.k.a. Tornadoes, "*That* Time of the Month, "The Cleaning Lady," "The Rag," "Monthly Bill," "Why-didn't-my-dad-ever-tell-me-about-this?" etc.

PMS

A slick marketing slogan which the advertising gurus use to sell various feminine products. I think it is supposed to mean "Pre-Menstrual Syndrome," but every woman I have ever met, or any man that has ever experienced his wife's rough periods, uses this word whether it's "Pre-," "Mid-," or "Post-" menstrual symptoms.

"Speed" Terms to Know

Wind Speed is the strength of the wind in the storm, which determines how much destruction it will cause.

Storm Speed is how fast the storm is moving, or how long it will hang over you and kick your butt. In other words, if you have to have high winds, pray for a fast storm.

"Tidal" Terms to Know

Tidal Surge: a slow moving storm surge which causes flooding and widespread damage because it keeping coming and coming and coming. It will get your butt wet.

Tidal Wave: enough water to flood you like a tidal flow, but coming at you fast enough to cause severe damage if you a too close. It will knock you on your butt.

Tsunami: the mother of all tidal waves. You are history if you are anywhere close. It will tear your butt off.

Tornado Country
Within 100 feet of any woman who experiences monthly periods.

Tornado Season
Anytime after a woman experiences her first period until menopause kicks in.

Tornado Warning
Approximately 21 days since the last period. By this time, you know if it's a good month or a bad month.

Tornado Watch
Starts approximately 18 days after the end of her last period, which is really about 3 days before the next period "starts" (hence, the need for feminine products), and usually when

the dreaded "PMS" symptoms start to appear on the horizon (if they are going to appear that month).

Waterspout
The equivalent of a tornado, but over water...and just when you thought you were safe!

FREQUENTLY ASKED
(BUT STUPID) QUESTIONS

What's a hurricane got to do with menopause?
    Clearly, the poor fool who asked this question does not have a menopausal wife and has no idea what is coming his way.

What are the "usual products" you buy at the store once a month?
    Clearly, this question is being asked by some nosey pre-teen boy with no older sisters.

How do I know when to run and hide, and when to stand up to a hurricane?
    First, experience. Like the country song says: "You gotta know when to hold 'em; know

when to fold 'em; know when to walk away; and know when to run."

Second, you don't! It's all a mix of guessing, men's intuition (an oxymoron, if I ever heard one), and being slammed enough you just can't take it anymore. You should have caught this last tip in Chapter 11, so maybe you'd better read it again.

How dare you say such mean things in this book about your wife! What gives you the right?

Uh, oh. Someone else's wife is reading this book.

EVACUATION ROUTES and DESTINATIONS

ROUTES
- Any way you can, as fast as you can.

DESTINATIONS
- The Car, or "Accidentally" Leaving Your Phone at Home
- Any Bathroom with a Loud Fan
- The Shower, if the Bathroom has a Lock
- Off-site Meetings for Work

- Loud Sporting Events (especially if your kids are playing)
- Urgent Meetings at Work
- Loud Construction Sites

IF YOU CAN'T ESCAPE
- Follow the instructions of the old A-Bomb posters: Get on the floor, put your head between your legs, and kiss your ass goodbye.

SURVIVAL CHECKLIST

1. **Midol** (just in case she runs out). Put some in each car and in each bathroom.
2. **Migraine headache medication** (for YOU, just in case you forget to buy the Midol).
3. **A strong laxative,** or food that messes up your stomach, so you can legitimately spend more time in the bathroom <u>with</u> the fan on during those "special days." Oh, and don't forget to hide a few of your favorite magazines in the john for your reading pleasure...and a copy of this book!

4. **Inconspicuous earplugs**: If you can't find them, DON'T take the risk of using an unproven substitute.

5. **Wet-suit**: Keeps you warm when your wife has the night sweats. If you just wear flannels, they get wet and stay wet, so that doesn't work. But a wet suit will use your wife's perspiration to create a layer of warmed-up night sweat sealed in next to your body, so you won't get the chills.

6. **Dyn-O-Gel**: Don't we wish? (If you didn't "get" this one, go back to Chapter 10!)

7. **Emergency cash**: When buying anything for her, only the best will do. (Actually, it will save your hide). Remember, this money is not for YOU. I know it's tempting, but trust me, when you REALLY need to appease her with something nice, and you find out you've spent all your stash cash, you will regret the day.

8. **One round-trip plane ticket**, good anywhere, any time. Any questions?

HOW TO PREPARE
BEFORE HURRICANE SEASON HITS

Here's the rest of what the National Weather Service says about learning how to better co-exist with hurricanes, followed by my application to menopause and marriage. I think it is fair to say that these tips apply to all you younger men who have not yet experienced the full fury of Mother Nature:

Build stronger homes.

Don't just build your body up or your career, but build up your home. Build up your wife. Invest in her. Love her. Value her. Consider her feelings BEFORE you make big decisions. In fact, involve her in ALL of those kinds of decisions. And remember, she may tell you it's okay, when it's really not. Learn to read FEELINGS, not just process WORDS. Look through some women's magazines NOW, while you are young and not after your butt has been kicked.

Save up so you can rebuild after the storms.

If you know the storms are coming, save up for them so you won't be as upset when they hit. In this case, saving up could mean a number of things. It could mean cutting down a little on the expense of a hobby and having some money saved up for a special emergency vacation or gift. It also means saving up emotionally so you can better mend hurts. Do things for her for no other reason than that you love her (okay, and maybe for the hidden agenda of knowing those nice things will pay off later on!)

Become better educated.

Don't just say: "It won't happen to me." Learn about the symptoms. Learn about the pros and cons of different solutions. Talk about it together BEFORE it happens, so neither of you are caught off guard. Don't let the curse of being silent be passed on to any other generations. Start a "Men-On-Pause Support Group" in your neighborhood.